For Leah.

The Best In Me

Here's to changing the
world one poem at a time.
I look forward to our
future collaborations.

Ni K. B

7/15

The Best In Me

My Personal Success Journal

When passion is the piper

That you pay with your persistence

The path that you pursue

Need not be one of least resistance

Nicholas K. Buggs

Thank You

Thank you to my friends and family who continue to support me on this poetic and inspirational journey. Who I am and what I do could not be possible without you. The love I share through my words is merely a reflection of the love that you have shown me. Please consider this to be my way of paying it forward.

Introduction

Throughout this journal, I will provide you with inspirational and motivational messages designed to help you focus on the positive behaviors that will lead you on your way to personal success. It has often been said that "what you believe, you can achieve" and I am a firm believer in that. The actions that you take day in and day out to achieve your goals are the direct result of your mindset. A positive mindset yields positive results while a negative mindset yields negative results. It is by continuously focusing on the positive in any and every situation that you will overcome your obstacles and take the necessary actions to achieve success.

Step 1: Reflection

To help you on your way, each inspirational message in this journal is accompanied by an opportunity for you to reflect on what those words mean to you. After all, it is not enough to simply read the words; you must connect and identify with the words as well. By blending each message with your own personal feelings, you can see yourself in the words. This is why we call it a **Reflection**.

Your reflection is not only who you are today, but it is also the person that you wish to be. As you read each message, think about how you want to live your life. Think about the behaviors over which you need to take control. Think about the negatives that you need to turn into positives and use this opportunity to tell yourself who you want to become:

"I need to stop being so negative. I need to be more positive."

"I need to stop procrastinating. I need to set goals and take immediate action."

"I need to stop letting other people control me. I need to take ownership of my life."

Taking time for personal reflection each week offers you an opportunity to be honest with yourself. It is not about who you are pretending to be; it is about who you are and who you *know* you can be. Try your best to make this connection and you will be one step closer to reaching your goals.

Step 2: Obstacles

Once you have taken the opportunity to make a personal connection with each message, you will then be asked to describe the **Obstacles** that are preventing you (or could prevent you) from being the person you wish to be. The goal here is to recognize the internal and external influences that can impact your ability to be successful.

Internal influences are those that you inflict upon yourself such as self-doubt or a lack of confidence. You may not know it yet, but these are the influences over which you have the most control. In order to take back that control, you simply need to take the time to train your mind to believe that you are better than these negatives.

External influences are those that come from your environment and the people within it. These influences could include friends, family, or coworkers with negative intentions demonstrated through their actions or their words. Though you do not have complete control over these influences, you do have control over how you permit those influences to affect you. When speaking on the subject of personal achievement, the author Napoleon Hill once said,

> "*There is nothing in this world that I can't do something about if it is nothing more than to adjust myself to an unpleasant situation so that it does not destroy my spirit.*"

In his autobiography, *The Greatest*, the great Muhammad Ali once wrote:

> "*It's funny, but those who hate me most sometimes inspire me the most.*"

The goal here is to never allow external influences to destroy your spirit, no matter how negative they may be. Instead, take control of your own feelings and protect them with everything you've got.

Step3: Plan

The final step you will take each week will be to create a **Plan** for what you hope to accomplish over the next seven days. This plan should be a list of real, actionable goals. These goals can include tangible things like:

"Read a book on personal achievement."

"Exercise for one hour every day."

"Make a thousand dollars in sales."

It can also include intangible things like:

"Don't listen to what *they* say."

"Keep a positive attitude towards all people."

"Finish what I started."

Once you set your plan, stick to it. Look at it every day if you have to. Just don't forget that it's not enough to simply want something or even to plan for it; if you truly want it, you have to work for it.

"Nothing of value comes without being earned. That's why great leaders are those who lead by example first..."

~ Michael Jordan

"I have not failed. I've just found 10,000 ways that won't work."

~ Thomas Edison

The next 52 weeks are yours for the taking, so make the most of each and every one. I hope that my words can offer the right amount of inspiration to keep you moving in the right direction but, in the end, your success depends on you. **Good luck!**

Foreword

I am poetry in motion
But can make the time stand still
I am memories and feelings
I am dreams yet unfulfilled
I am lessons learned from living
That for many will ring true
I am inspired to inspire
And my inspiration's you

~ Nicholas K. Buggs

Don't forget your pencil.

This Journal Belongs To

_____

Name

_____

Date

By the end of this year, I will:

_____

_____

_____

Week 1: Learn To Be Happy

When you learn how to be happy
Then nothing else will do
And you won't let anyone else
Take that away from you
And if anyone around you
Should even think to try
There's one thing you should tell them
In a word, just say, "Goodbye"

Protect your happiness from those who would think to take it away from you.

It belongs to you and no one else.

Reflection (How do you relate to this message?)

_____

_____

_____

_____

_____

Obstacles (What is standing in your way?)

_____

_____

_____

_____

Plan (What will you accomplish this week?)

_____

_____

_____

_____

_____

Week 2: Dance

Dance like no one's looking
Dance the night away
Dance to your own music
Don't care what people say
Dance to your own heartbeat
Hear the sound from deep within
Dance to free your heart and soul
And love the skin you're in

Choose your own path.

Do not let others choose it for you.

Reflection (How do you relate to this message?)

_____

_____

_____

_____

_____

Obstacles (What is standing in your way?)

_____

_____

_____

_____

Plan (What will you accomplish this week?)

_____

_____

_____

_____

Week 3: Work In Progress

I'm still a work in progress
And just knowing that can hurt
For knowing that I'm not my best
Can make me feel my worst
But quiet meditation
Alone here in my bed
Helps me to remain focused
On the journey still ahead

We are all a work in progress. Instead of dwelling on what we have not accomplished, we should take time to focus on what we are doing to bring our dreams to life. We don't get there through perfection; we get there through persistence.

Reflection (How do you relate to this message?)

_____

_____

_____

_____

_____

Obstacles (What is standing in your way?)

_____

_____

_____

_____

Plan (What will you accomplish this week?)

_____

_____

_____

_____

_____

Week 4: Be

Wake up in the morning
And be who you want to be
It's not enough to think it
Or to simply just believe
And even if you're not quite there
Just know you're on your way
For who you'll be tomorrow
Starts with who you are today

Believing in yourself is only the first step. Once you
believe, you must become the person you believe in.

Don't just think it. Be it.

Reflection (How do you relate to this message?)

_____

_____

_____

_____

_____

Obstacles (What is standing in your way?)

_____

_____

_____

_____

_____

Plan (What will you accomplish this week?)

_____

_____

_____

_____

_____

Week 5: The Journey

Remember just how far you've come
Fear not the journey's length
Take pride in everything you've done
And know you have the strength
Of what now lies ahead of you
There's no need to be scared
You've worked so hard to get here
Just know that you're prepared

Your journey can be long and hard. Don't give up.
Everything that you have gone through has prepared
you for what lies ahead. Don't be afraid.

You are prepared.

Reflection (How do you relate to this message?)

_____

_____

_____

_____

_____

Obstacles (What is standing in your way?)

_____

_____

_____

_____

Plan (What will you accomplish this week?)

_____

_____

_____

_____

Week 6: Concentrate

Concentrate on what you want
Believe it will be yours
If the window of opportunity's locked
Then knock on every door
For if you want to reach your goals
Your focus must be clear
So concentrate on what you want
And soon it will be here

It is not what we want in life that we achieve. We achieve that which we desire with such passion that our minds remain focused upon it and our bodies carry out the actions necessary to bring it into reality.

Reflection (How do you relate to this message?)

_____

_____

_____

_____

_____

Obstacles (What is standing in your way?)

_____

_____

_____

_____

_____

Plan (What will you accomplish this week?)

_____

_____

_____

_____

_____

Week 7: Architect

I'm the architect of my future
The blueprint's in my hands
I've taken all my hopes and dreams
And turned them into plans
For I will build a future
That's by my own design
So I will be the architect
'Til victory is mine

You must turn your desires into plans and turn those plans into actions. This is the foundation upon which your success will be built.

Reflection (How do you relate to this message?)

_____

_____

_____

_____

_____

Obstacles (What is standing in your way?)

_____

_____

_____

_____

_____

Plan (What will you accomplish this week?)

_____

_____

_____

_____

_____

Week 8: Hardcore

I believe in the struggle
In the pain and the gain
I believe in the fight
Through the stress and the strain
I'll do what it takes
And then do some more
You'd better believe
That I am hardcore

Progress is never easy. It is your willingness and ability to keep fighting that will keep you moving forward. If you want it badly enough, you are going to have to work hard for it.

Reflection (How do you relate to this message?)

_____

_____

_____

_____

_____

Obstacles (What is standing in your way?)

_____

_____

_____

_____

_____

Plan (What will you accomplish this week?)

_____

_____

_____

_____

_____

Week 9: Fear of Failure

I open up my heart to you
So you will know the truth
That fearing failure doesn't work
And I am living proof
For failure only happens
If you're choosing to give in
If you're open to what's possible
Then one day you will win

Failure is inevitable but it is not an absolute. Failure is going to happen. It's what you do next that matters.

Reflection (How do you relate to this message?)

_____

_____

_____

_____

_____

Obstacles (What is standing in your way?)

_____

_____

_____

_____

_____

Plan (What will you accomplish this week?)

_____

_____

_____

_____

_____

Week 10: Tomorrow

I love the possibilities
The unknown fuels my fire
I look forward to what life may bring
When driven by desire
Tomorrow's filled with all the things
That I still haven't done
So I can say with confidence
The best has yet to come

If you believe in ALL of the possibilities, you will come to realize that there is no single path to success. What you have in mind today may not be the road you take in the end. Expect and embrace the unexpected.

Reflection (How do you relate to this message?)

_____

_____

_____

_____

_____

Obstacles (What is standing in your way?)

_____

_____

_____

_____

Plan (What will you accomplish this week?)

_____

_____

_____

_____

_____

Week 11: Hush

If you have nothing good to say
Then say nothing at all
If you're not here to lift me up
You're here to watch me fall
But I won't let you trip me up
In public or in private
So my friendly advice to you
Is learn how to be quiet

Shut out the negative influences in your life. Each one is like a chain around your feet tying you down to the present or pulling you back into your past. If you want to move forward, you can no longer listen to "them". They don't want the same things you do.

Reflection (How do you relate to this message?)

_____

_____

_____

_____

_____

Obstacles (What is standing in your way?)

_____

_____

_____

_____

_____

Plan (What will you accomplish this week?)

_____

_____

_____

_____

_____

Week 12: Flawless

Flawless I will never be
Perfection is a myth
So I don't focus on my flaws
I focus on my gifts
So when you see me strut my stuff
Please do not think me vain
I'm celebrating who I am
And you should do the same

Be proud of who you are and what you are working to accomplish. It's not about being perfect; it's about being the best you that you can be.

Reflection (How do you relate to this message?)

_____

_____

_____

_____

_____

Obstacles (What is standing in your way?)

_____

_____

_____

_____

_____

Plan (What will you accomplish this week?)

_____

_____

_____

_____

_____

Week 13: Enthusiasm

Be enthusiastic
In everything you do
Don't deny your passion
Allow it to shine through
For in passion you'll find purpose
And soon you're bound to see
That once you find your passion
There is nothing you can't be

If you want something badly enough, it should show in everything you do. When your desire becomes an obsession, you know you are on your way.

Reflection (How do you relate to this message?)

_____

_____

_____

_____

_____

Obstacles (What is standing in your way?)

_____

_____

_____

_____

_____

Plan (What will you accomplish this week?)

_____

_____

_____

_____

_____

Week 14: Payoff

In the moment that you realize
Your hard work has paid off
You see everything was worth it
Every victory every loss
But long before you get there
You only see what need be done
But in those moments rest assured
That soon your day will come

Never lose sight of what you are working towards. If you remain focused on your goal, you'll know that every step you take will be worth it in the end.

Reflection (How do you relate to this message?)

_____

_____

_____

_____

Obstacles (What is standing in your way?)

_____

_____

_____

_____

Plan (What will you accomplish this week?)

_____

_____

_____

_____

Week 15: Funny Stuff

Some people talk behind my back
As if they're judge and jury
But they don't even know me so
Their vision's kind of blurry
They talk about me like they know
But they don't know the half
So when I hear them whispering
Then I can't help but laugh

When others choose to judge you (and they will), don't take their criticism to heart.

Reflection (How do you relate to this message?)

_____

_____

_____

_____

_____

Obstacles (What is standing in your way?)

_____

_____

_____

_____

_____

Plan (What will you accomplish this week?)

_____

_____

_____

_____

_____

Week 16: The Chase

When I was young they told me
That I should follow my dreams
But that was not the best advice
No matter how good it seemed
For if you simply follow dreams
They may leave you behind
So instead I choose to chase my dreams
Until I've made them mine

Ready. Set. Go!

Chase your dreams. After all, they're not going to sit
around all day waiting for you.

Reflection (How do you relate to this message?)

_____

_____

_____

_____

_____

Obstacles (What is standing in your way?)

_____

_____

_____

_____

_____

Plan (What will you accomplish this week?)

_____

_____

_____

_____

_____

Week 17: Misguided Love

It's not that they hate you
It's that they hate that they love you
Even when you're on top
They still think they're above you
And despite the hard work
The haters still have the nerve
To think all that you've got
Is something you don't deserve
So when you're on top
You should look down and tell them
There's no hate in your heart
Then just reach out to help them
For they'll learn to love you
No matter how hard they fight it
Because the truth in the end
Hate is just love misguided

Other people's hate is not an invitation for you to do the same. They are simply crying out for the love that is missing from their hearts.

Reflection (How do you relate to this message?)

_____

_____

_____

_____

_____

Obstacles (What is standing in your way?)

_____

_____

_____

_____

Plan (What will you accomplish this week?)

_____

_____

_____

_____

Week 18: Negative

A negative will be defined
By the way you choose to see it
But a positive is what you'll see
If you simply choose to be it

Search for the positive in every situation. There is almost always something you can find. Hold on to that and the negative will soon fade away.

Remember: Negativity takes away but positivity will always give back.

Reflection (How do you relate to this message?)

_____

_____

_____

_____

_____

Obstacles (What is standing in your way?)

_____

_____

_____

_____

Plan (What will you accomplish this week?)

_____

_____

_____

_____

Week 19: Music

I'm focused in this moment
I have to keep control
I have to quench the fire
That is burning in my soul
And as I look within myself
To find my inner peace
I listen to the music
That soothes the savage beast

Music can be the soundtrack to our lives. Listen to the music that echoes the feelings and emotions that you desire and it will create harmony with your dreams.

Reflection (How do you relate to this message?)

_____

_____

_____

_____

_____

Obstacles (What is standing in your way?)

_____

_____

_____

_____

_____

Plan (What will you accomplish this week?)

_____

_____

_____

_____

_____

Week 20: 4%

What if you learned that 4%
Was all that it would take
To make all of the progress
That you wished that you could make
And what if just that 4%
Was key to your success
Would you be willing to give 4%
Or would you give it less
And what if 4% is all
That's standing in your way
Would you give it knowing 4%
Is one hour a day?

Don't try to find time to pursue your dreams; make time. 4% is only an hour a day. Are you willing to give 4% for what you want in life?

Reflection (How do you relate to this message?)

_____

_____

_____

_____

_____

Obstacles (What is standing in your way?)

_____

_____

_____

_____

_____

Plan (What will you accomplish this week?)

_____

_____

_____

_____

_____

Week 21: Top of the World

Just because I'm on top of the world
Doesn't mean that I'm above you
And just because you don't know my name
Doesn't mean that I don't love you
And just because from where I stand
I have a different view
It doesn't mean I have the right
To look down upon you

As you begin to reap the results of your hard work and dedication, you may find yourself in a different social or financial standing than others around you. What you have today doesn't make you any better than anyone else. It's what you give that matters.

Reflection (How do you relate to this message?)

_____

_____

_____

_____

Obstacles (What is standing in your way?)

_____

_____

_____

_____

Plan (What will you accomplish this week?)

_____

_____

_____

_____

Week 22: Mud and Scars

Give me mud
And give me scars
I don't waste dreams
On shooting stars
Give me grit
And give me grime
I don't need glitter
To make me shine

Are you willing to go through the dirt to become a flower? You have to be willing to do the hard work if you want to succeed. Don't wish; work hard.

Reflection (How do you relate to this message?)

_____

_____

_____

_____

_____

Obstacles (What is standing in your way?)

_____

_____

_____

_____

_____

Plan (What will you accomplish this week?)

_____

_____

_____

_____

_____

Week 23: I May Fall

If there's one thing I know
I fall but I grow
Like the leaves of a tree
I've learned to let go
For when one season ends
Another begins
And the days that have passed
Are gone with the wind
So I embrace the new season
And whatever it brings
Even the darkest of winters
Must give way to Spring

Learn to let go of the things that you can't control.
Your past is behind you now and it's time to look
forward to your future. The darkness always gives way
to the light.

Reflection (How do you relate to this message?)

_____

_____

_____

_____

_____

Obstacles (What is standing in your way?)

_____

_____

_____

_____

_____

Plan (What will you accomplish this week?)

_____

_____

_____

_____

_____

Week 24: The Best Medicine

Laughter is my medicine
I've found that it's the cure
I use it to heal everything
That I just might endure
And if I ever feel that stress
Is getting in the way
There's nothing like some laughter
To make it go away

It's not all about the hard work. You have to learn to enjoy yourself along the way. Laugh with friends, eat with family, and share memories with loved ones.

Reflection (How do you relate to this message?)

_____

_____

_____

_____

_____

Obstacles (What is standing in your way?)

_____

_____

_____

_____

_____

Plan (What will you accomplish this week?)

_____

_____

_____

_____

_____

Week 25: Reach for the Sun

What if the sun
Was an arm's length away
Would you try to reach out
And capture the day
Or would you be afraid
That you would get burned
With fear in your heart
From your life's lessons learned
For if the sun sets
Your chance will pass by
And the sun will return
To its place in the sky

What you could not do yesterday does not define what you can do today. Don't be afraid to take a chance and reach out for what you want. Learn from your past; don't fear it.

Reflection (How do you relate to this message?)

_____

_____

_____

_____

_____

Obstacles (What is standing in your way?)

_____

_____

_____

_____

Plan (What will you accomplish this week?)

_____

_____

_____

_____

Week 26: Free Your Mind

Free your mind of the negative
Let the positive remain
For if your mind is not set free
Your sprit will be drained
Our bodies are the vessels
Through which our spirits shine
But we won't get to see the light
If we don't clear our minds

Take some time out to clear your mind and regain your focus. It's impossible to see the forest when you're living amongst the trees.

Reflection (How do you relate to this message?)

_____

_____

_____

_____

Obstacles (What is standing in your way?)

_____

_____

_____

_____

Plan (What will you accomplish this week?)

_____

_____

_____

_____

Week 27: Prince and the Pauper

Imagine if you met the person
That you were going to be
Would you turn your life around
And live it differently
Or would you stay upon your path
And make the same mistakes
Would you gamble with your future
And take chances with your fate
To those who say they'd make the change
I'd say I'm not convinced
Though this could be the difference
Between the pauper and the prince

Look at the path you are on. Are you doing the right
things to get you to where you want to be in life? If
not, there's no better time than now to change course.

Reflection (How do you relate to this message?)

_____

_____

_____

_____

_____

Obstacles (What is standing in your way?)

_____

_____

_____

_____

Plan (What will you accomplish this week?)

_____

_____

_____

_____

_____

Week 28: Visualize

See yourself with what you want
Believe it will be yours
Move mountains with your mind and know
That there are no closed doors
So when you get what it is you want
Let it come as no surprise
There's nothing that's beyond your reach
If you first visualize

If you want something badly enough, begin to visualize yourself in possession of it. Once you believe in your heart that it is yours, your mind won't accept any other outcome.

Reflection (How do you relate to this message?)

_____

_____

_____

_____

_____

Obstacles (What is standing in your way?)

_____

_____

_____

_____

_____

Plan (What will you accomplish this week?)

_____

_____

_____

_____

_____

Week 29: Opportunity

For the window of opportunity
He searched and searched some more
But never did he realize
The window was a door

Don't get caught up in doing the same things over and over again expecting a different result. Look at things from a new perspective and find a new approach. You never know, it could be right in front of your nose.

Reflection (How do you relate to this message?)

_____

_____

_____

_____

_____

Obstacles (What is standing in your way?)

_____

_____

_____

_____

_____

Plan (What will you accomplish this week?)

_____

_____

_____

_____

_____

Week 30: Thoughts

Try to keep the negative thoughts
Buried in your head
These are things that can be thought
But never should be said
For who you are is not defined
By thoughts left in your head
Who you are will be defined
By what you do instead

Don't speak things into existence that don't have a positive impact on yourself and those around you. We all have negative thoughts from time to time. Just try your best not to become the negativity that you feel.

Reflection (How do you relate to this message?)

_____

_____

_____

_____

_____

Obstacles (What is standing in your way?)

_____

_____

_____

_____

Plan (What will you accomplish this week?)

_____

_____

_____

_____

_____

Week 31: Take Time

Take a second to smile
Take a minute to laugh
Take an hour to think
About all that you have
Take a day for yourself
Take a weekend away
Take a week off from work
To just go out and play
For time's of the essence
The essence of life
Just remember to take it
And you'll be alright

Don't become so focused on your dreams that you forget about your life. Smile, laugh, love, and enjoy every day. Take time for yourself or you'll watch as it slips right out of your hands.

Reflection (How do you relate to this message?)

_____

_____

_____

_____

Obstacles (What is standing in your way?)

_____

_____

_____

_____

Plan (What will you accomplish this week?)

_____

_____

_____

_____

Week 32: My Own Hero

There's no cage that can hold me
No wall I can't climb
There's nothing I want
That cannot be mine
No roadblock can stop me
No hurdle too high
I'll step on the clouds
As I reach for the sky
For I am determined
I will persevere
I am my own hero
So there's nothing to fear

Believe in yourself. Know that you can accomplish
anything that you set your heart, mind, and energy to.

Reflection (How do you relate to this message?)

_____

_____

_____

_____

_____

Obstacles (What is standing in your way?)

_____

_____

_____

_____

_____

Plan (What will you accomplish this week?)

_____

_____

_____

_____

_____

Week 33: The View From Here

The view from here is beautiful
Though you may not believe it
For what I see's amazing
Though you may not yet see it
For what I see is progress
From where I used to be
And there can be no better view
Than to view a better me

Reflect on the progress you've made and realize just how far you've come. You may not be where you want to be, but you are definitely not where you were.

Reflection (How do you relate to this message?)

_____

_____

_____

_____

_____

Obstacles (What is standing in your way?)

_____

_____

_____

_____

_____

Plan (What will you accomplish this week?)

_____

_____

_____

_____

_____

Week 34: Suffer

Don't suffer in the darkness
Let the light shine on your pain
And allow all of your suffering
To fuel your drive to change
For to be the type of person
That you now wish to be
Don't be afraid to suffer
For one day you'll succeed

Do not suffer in your current situation. Instead, turn that suffering into a burning desire to make the progress you need to reach your goals.

If where you are is not where you were meant to be, it's time to move in a new direction.

Reflection (How do you relate to this message?)

_____

_____

_____

_____

_____

Obstacles (What is standing in your way?)

_____

_____

_____

_____

_____

Plan (What will you accomplish this week?)

_____

_____

_____

_____

_____

Week 35: Hi

I'd like to introduce myself
I hope that that's alright
No longer in the shadows
I now step into the light
I have so much to offer
There's no sense in being shy
So I'll take this opportunity
To simply just say hi

You can't chase your dreams while hiding in the shadows. Come out into the open and have the confidence to go for what you want. Introduce yourself to the world. It can't wait to meet you!

Reflection (How do you relate to this message?)

_____

_____

_____

_____

_____

Obstacles (What is standing in your way?)

_____

_____

_____

_____

Plan (What will you accomplish this week?)

_____

_____

_____

_____

_____

Week 36: Binoculars

Where is it you see yourself
When you look to days ahead
Will you be right where you are
Or somewhere else instead
Can you see all of your dreams
Just over the hill
And are you out there chasing them
Or are you standing still
This vision of your future
That you should try to see
Will give you true perspective
Of where you want to be
So look out in the distance
And see with your own eyes
All the possibilities
You might just be surprised

Do you know exactly where you want to be in the future? It's not enough to simply want to be successful; you have to know what success looks like. That's the dream that you chase.

Reflection (How do you relate to this message?)

_____

_____

_____

_____

_____

Obstacles (What is standing in your way?)

_____

_____

_____

_____

Plan (What will you accomplish this week?)

_____

_____

_____

_____

Week 37: Bend

Bend in case the wind should blow
And sway there in the breeze
Adapt to your surroundings
To place your mind at ease
For if you let these words define
The choices that you make
Then even in those trying times
You'll bend but never break

Be ready to adapt to what your journey may bring. No one's path is straight and narrow or without obstacles and speed bumps. Expect the unexpected and be willing to change course when you need to.

Reflection (How do you relate to this message?)

_____

_____

_____

_____

_____

Obstacles (What is standing in your way?)

_____

_____

_____

_____

Plan (What will you accomplish this week?)

_____

_____

_____

_____

Week 38: Illusion

Limits like fears
Are just an illusion
They cloud up your mind
And lead to confusion
To break through your limits
And conquer your fears
You must be prepared
For blood, sweat, and tears
For dreams are just wishes
You make while asleep
But goals are achieved
By moving your feet

Your limits are defined by fears and self-doubt. Don't limit your potential by believing in what you can't do. Expand your opportunities by believing in what you can do.

Reflection (How do you relate to this message?)

_____

_____

_____

_____

_____

Obstacles (What is standing in your way?)

_____

_____

_____

_____

Plan (What will you accomplish this week?)

_____

_____

_____

_____

Week 39: Pay the Piper

When passion is the piper
That you pay with your persistence
The path that you pursue
Need not be one of least resistance

Persistence driven by passion is the driving force behind any success. There will always be resistance along the path to great achievement. It is your persistence that will help you to overcome your obstacles on the way to realizing your dreams.

Reflection (How do you relate to this message?)

_____

_____

_____

_____

_____

Obstacles (What is standing in your way?)

_____

_____

_____

_____

_____

Plan (What will you accomplish this week?)

_____

_____

_____

_____

_____

Week 40: In the Mirror

When I look in the mirror
There's one thing I see
When I look in the mirror
I only see me
When I look in the mirror
I don't see the don'ts
I don't see the shouldn'ts
Or the can'ts or the won'ts
When I look in the mirror
I see all I can be
And the me that I see
I am so proud to be

What do you see when you look in the mirror? Do you see the scars of days passed or do you see the potential of the future to come? Do you see your flaws and imperfections or do you see the gifts that you have to share with the world? Be proud of what you see today and be hopeful for what you are becoming.

Reflection (How do you relate to this message?)

_____

_____

_____

_____

_____

Obstacles (What is standing in your way?)

_____

_____

_____

_____

_____

Plan (What will you accomplish this week?)

_____

_____

_____

_____

_____

Week 41: If

You'll only learn your lesson
If you're willing to be taught
And you'll only gain new knowledge
If you're open to new thoughts
You'll only keep your freedom
If you're not willing to be bought
And you'll never know just if you can
If you think that you cannot

Approach life (and the people you meet) with an open mind and an open heart. These are the windows of opportunity. Don't ever close them.

Reflection (How do you relate to this message?)

_____

_____

_____

_____

Obstacles (What is standing in your way?)

_____

_____

_____

_____

Plan (What will you accomplish this week?)

_____

_____

_____

_____

Week 42: Possibility

It's the possibility that keeps me going
Not the guarantee
It's knowing that I've tried my best
That lets my soul run free
For if my dreams were guaranteed
There'd be no need to try
For even birds must learn to walk
Before they learn to fly

Nothing is guaranteed. Just as a bird will never fly if it doesn't spread its wings, you will never know success if you don't try your best.

Your potential is within you, but your dreams will leave without you if you don't move your feet.

Reflection (How do you relate to this message?)

_____

_____

_____

_____

_____

Obstacles (What is standing in your way?)

_____

_____

_____

_____

Plan (What will you accomplish this week?)

_____

_____

_____

_____

_____

Week 43: Shine

There's no weakness in this moment
So please don't be deceived
For it was in the darkness
That light was first conceived
So even in the darkness
I'll make this moment mine
For it is in the darkness
That I will choose to shine

It's not the moment that defines us; it's what we do in that moment that defines us. Darkness is sure to come and our fears and our failures will cast shadows on our paths. When those days come, light your path with the faith you have in all that you can achieve. No pitch of darkness can ever hold back the light.

Don't forget to shine!

Reflection (How do you relate to this message?)

_____

_____

_____

_____

Obstacles (What is standing in your way?)

_____

_____

_____

_____

Plan (What will you accomplish this week?)

_____

_____

_____

_____

Week 44: Can't

Can't is subjective
And has no objective
If you think that you can't
Then change your perspective

What is the point in saying you can't?

Why defeat yourself before you've given yourself a chance? Why limit yourself based on past failures instead of believing in future possibilities?

"Can't" is a perspective and only lives in the now. Don't let it define where you're going (or not).

Reflection (How do you relate to this message?)

_____

_____

_____

_____

_____

Obstacles (What is standing in your way?)

_____

_____

_____

_____

Plan (What will you accomplish this week?)

_____

_____

_____

_____

_____

Week 45: Proud

I'm proud of everything you've done
You've come so very far
Just imagine where you've been
And look at where you are
For all that you've accomplished
Is just like a dream come true
And though I've said it once before
I'm so proud of you!

Look at yourself in the mirror and repeat those words. It's ok. It's not silly or stupid. It's an affirmation of the love and pride you have for yourself. After all, you have to love and appreciate yourself before you can expect anyone else to.

Reflection (How do you relate to this message?)

_____

_____

_____

_____

_____

Obstacles (What is standing in your way?)

_____

_____

_____

_____

Plan (What will you accomplish this week?)

_____

_____

_____

_____

_____

Week 46: Giant Leap

They said I should take baby steps
That progress comes in time
But baby steps were just too slow
For what I had in mind
So I made myself a promise
And it's a promise I still keep
That instead of taking baby steps
I'll take a giant leap

Sometimes you need to take risks. Sometimes you need to take chances. Don't be afraid to throw caution to the wind and take a giant leap towards your goals.

Reflection (How do you relate to this message?)

_____

_____

_____

_____

Obstacles (What is standing in your way?)

_____

_____

_____

_____

Plan (What will you accomplish this week?)

_____

_____

_____

_____

Week 47: Move Your Feet

You'll make no progress
Standing still
For potential can
But never will
And without action
No plan's complete
So make the choice
To move your feet

It is true that you should have a plan, but don't work so hard on the plan that you never take action. Take the plan that you have and move forward. Learn along the way and refine your plan as you go. A plan with no action is like potential without reward. There is no value in it.

Reflection (How do you relate to this message?)

_____

_____

_____

_____

_____

Obstacles (What is standing in your way?)

_____

_____

_____

_____

Plan (What will you accomplish this week?)

_____

_____

_____

_____

_____

Week 48: Directions

Directions can be followed
To places that are known
But if you're trying to find yourself
You'll have to find it on your own

You can follow others to better yourself, but you can't follow others to be yourself. Learn from others, but find your own path.

Reflection (How do you relate to this message?)

_____

_____

_____

_____

_____

Obstacles (What is standing in your way?)

_____

_____

_____

_____

_____

Plan (What will you accomplish this week?)

_____

_____

_____

_____

_____

Week 49: Anything You Can Do

Anything you can do
I say whatever
For whatever you can do
Won't make me better
And the best of what I can do
I've yet to see
So I hope you won't mind
If I focus on me

Don't be distracted by those who brag about what they have. It is not those who show their success that you should admire; it is those who share their success that you should admire instead.

Reflection (How do you relate to this message?)

_____

_____

_____

_____

Obstacles (What is standing in your way?)

_____

_____

_____

_____

Plan (What will you accomplish this week?)

_____

_____

_____

_____

Week 50: Choices

Whenever people ask you why
You do the things you do
Just turn around and ask them why
They wouldn't do it too
And when they give excuses
That just don't hold any weight
You can just remind them
They are masters of their fate

When people question your dedication and call it an obsession, remember that this is your journey, not theirs. Continue on the path that you have forged for yourself. You are the master of your fate.

Reflection (How do you relate to this message?)

_____

_____

_____

_____

_____

Obstacles (What is standing in your way?)

_____

_____

_____

_____

_____

Plan (What will you accomplish this week?)

_____

_____

_____

_____

_____

Week 51: Take Control

Be FAST enough to win the race
But smart enough to mind your pace
Be TRANSFORMED to something new
As long as it's a better you
Be STRONG enough to overcome
But know your work is never done
Be POWERFUL in mind and flesh
And take control of your success

Take control of your success by becoming the person you want to be. Who you are defines what you do and how you do it.

Reflection (How do you relate to this message?)

_____

_____

_____

_____

_____

Obstacles (What is standing in your way?)

_____

_____

_____

_____

_____

Plan (What will you accomplish this week?)

_____

_____

_____

_____

_____

Week 52: In Flight

They said I needed wings to fly
But I suppose I didn't hear
I guess that they're not loud enough
To reach me way up here

What you have been able to accomplish this year has been the result of the faith that you have had in yourself and the belief that you can do anything you set your mind to.   You believed that you could fly and you flew.

Now, the only thing between you and your dreams is air and opportunity. Enjoy the flight!

Reflection (How do you relate to this message?)

_____

_____

_____

_____

Obstacles (What is standing in your way?)

_____

_____

_____

_____

Plan (What will you accomplish this week?)

_____

_____

_____

_____

I Kept My Promise

_____

Name

_____

Date

In one year, I accomplished:

_____

_____

_____

About the Author

Nicholas K. Buggs is a poet whose inspiration comes from real people just like you. Unlike most poets who provide their own perspectives on the world through their words, Nick draws upon the feelings and sentiments of individuals across the globe in an effort to translate their experiences into positive, inspirational messages.

Since March of 2014, Nick has written over 800 poems inspired by people that he has come across on Instagram through their likes and follows on his account (@nicks_words). In fact, every poem in this book was inspired by his Instagram likers and followers. This continuous pool of inspiration has led to a seemingly endless catalogue of poetry that continues to inspire and motivate more and more people every day.

If you would like to see more of his work, and see his real-life inspirations, feel free to follow **Nick's Words** on Instagram, Twitter, Facebook, and Pinterest. He also provides custom poetry as a gift or keepsake for every occasion through his website www.nickswords.com.

Pay It Forward

If you received this journal as a gift, please pay it forward.

Gift a copy to a friend, family member, coworker, or even a complete stranger. After all, everyone could use a little inspiration.

Purchase your gift copy on **amazon.com**.

Do whatever you can do
Knowing you can't do it all
For there's no act of kindness
That could ever be too small